Boyd's COMMENTARY STUDY NOTES

To be used as a workbook
for the Boyd's Commentary
and Sunday School Lessons

R.H. BOYD
EST. 1896

www.rhboyd.com

Copyright ©
R.H. Boyd Publishing Corporation
6717 Centennial Blvd.• Nashville, Tennessee 37209-1017

How to
Use This Book

Key Themes/Key Verse

Analyze what the Key Verse is saying by selecting or identifying the key words in the verse. Look at what those words mean and what they say to your understanding of the entire lesson.

Thoughts from the Text

You are encouraged to look closely at the biblical text and select at least three ideas which the text suggests. This section is expository in nature, as you let the Scriptures speak to you.

How Did This Lesson Impact My Life?

In this section, you are encouraged to write down those actions which you will take to show that this lesson has been understood and has relevancy for your life. This section allows you to take steps to make certain that the lesson does not remain lifeless bu that it come to a living reality in your experience.

Date: _____

Scripture Text:——————— Lesson Topic: _____

_____

_____

_____

Key Theme/Key Verse: _____

_____

_____

_____

_____

_____

Thoughts from the Text: _____

_____

_____

_____

_____

_____

How did this lesson impact my life?_____

_____

_____

_____

_____

_____

_____

1ST QUARTER

Date: _____

Scripture Text:——————— Lesson Topic: _____

_____
_____
_____

Key Theme/Key Verse: _____

_____
_____
_____
_____
_____

Thoughts from the Text: _____

_____
_____
_____
_____
_____

How did this lesson impact my life?_____

_____
_____
_____
_____
_____
_____

Date: _____

Scripture Text:——————— Lesson Topic: _____

_____
_____
_____

Key Theme/Key Verse: _____

_____
_____
_____
_____
_____

Thoughts from the Text: _____

_____
_____
_____
_____
_____

How did this lesson impact my life? _____

_____
_____
_____
_____
_____
_____

1ST QUARTER

Date: _____

Scripture Text:——————— Lesson Topic: _____

_____

_____

_____

Key Theme/Key Verse:_____

_____

_____

_____

_____

_____

Thoughts from the Text: _____

_____

_____

_____

_____

_____

How did this lesson impact my life?_____

_____

_____

_____

_____

_____

Date: _____

Scripture Text:————————— Lesson Topic: _____

_____

_____

_____

Key Theme/Key Verse:_____

_____

_____

_____

_____

_____

Thoughts from the Text: _____

_____

_____

_____

_____

_____

How did this lesson impact my life?_____

_____

_____

_____

_____

_____

_____

1ST QUARTER

Date: _____

Scripture Text:——————— Lesson Topic: _____

_____

_____

_____

Key Theme/Key Verse:_____

_____

_____

_____

_____

_____

Thoughts from the Text: _____

_____

_____

_____

_____

_____

How did this lesson impact my life?_____

_____

_____

_____

_____

_____

_____

Date: _____

Scripture Text:——————— Lesson Topic: _____

_____

_____

_____

Key Theme/Key Verse: _____

_____

_____

_____

_____

_____

Thoughts from the Text: _____

_____

_____

_____

_____

_____

How did this lesson impact my life?_____

_____

_____

_____

_____

_____

_____

Date: _____

Scripture Text:——————— Lesson Topic: _____

_____

_____

_____

Key Theme/Key Verse: _____

_____

_____

_____

_____

_____

Thoughts from the Text: _____

_____

_____

_____

_____

_____

How did this lesson impact my life?_____

_____

_____

_____

_____

_____

_____

Date: _____

Scripture Text:—————— Lesson Topic: _____

_____

_____

_____

Key Theme/Key Verse:_____

_____

_____

_____

_____

_____

Thoughts from the Text: _____

_____

_____

_____

_____

_____

How did this lesson impact my life?_____

_____

_____

_____

_____

_____

_____

1ST QUARTER

Date: _____

Scripture Text:————— Lesson Topic: _____

_____
_____
_____

Key Theme/Key Verse: _____

_____
_____
_____
_____
_____

Thoughts from the Text: _____

_____
_____
_____
_____
_____

How did this lesson impact my life?_____

_____
_____
_____
_____
_____
_____

Date: _____

Scripture Text:————————— Lesson Topic: _____

_____

_____

_____

Key Theme/Key Verse: _____

_____

_____

_____

_____

_____

Thoughts from the Text: _____

_____

_____

_____

_____

_____

How did this lesson impact my life? _____

_____

_____

_____

_____

_____

_____

1ST QUARTER

Date: _____

Scripture Text: —————— Lesson Topic: _____

_____

_____

_____

Key Theme/Key Verse: _____

_____

_____

_____

_____

_____

Thoughts from the Text: _____

_____

_____

_____

_____

_____

How did this lesson impact my life? _____

_____

_____

_____

_____

_____

_____

Date: _____

Scripture Text:——————— Lesson Topic: _____

_____

_____

_____

Key Theme/Key Verse: _____

_____

_____

_____

_____

Thoughts from the Text: _____

_____

_____

_____

_____

_____

How did this lesson impact my life? _____

_____

_____

_____

_____

_____

_____

NOTES

NOTES

2ND QUARTER

Date: _____

Scripture Text:—————— Lesson Topic: _____

_____

_____

_____

Key Theme/Key Verse:_____

_____

_____

_____

_____

_____

Thoughts from the Text: _____

_____

_____

_____

_____

_____

How did this lesson impact my life?_____

_____

_____

_____

_____

_____

_____

Date: _____

Scripture Text:————————— Lesson Topic: _____

_____

_____

_____

Key Theme/Key Verse: _____

_____

_____

_____

_____

_____

Thoughts from the Text: _____

_____

_____

_____

_____

_____

How did this lesson impact my life? _____

_____

_____

_____

_____

_____

_____

2ND QUARTER

Date: _____

Scripture Text:—————— Lesson Topic: _____

_____

_____

_____

Key Theme/Key Verse: _____

_____

_____

_____

_____

Thoughts from the Text: _____

_____

_____

_____

_____

_____

How did this lesson impact my life?_____

_____

_____

_____

_____

_____

Date: _____

Scripture Text:——————— Lesson Topic: _____

_____

_____

_____

Key Theme/Key Verse:_____

_____

_____

_____

_____

_____

Thoughts from the Text: _____

_____

_____

_____

_____

_____

How did this lesson impact my life?_____

_____

_____

_____

_____

_____

_____

Date: _____

Scripture Text:—————— Lesson Topic: _____

_____
_____
_____

Key Theme/Key Verse:_____

_____
_____
_____
_____
_____

Thoughts from the Text: _____

_____
_____
_____
_____
_____

How did this lesson impact my life?_____

_____
_____
_____
_____
_____
_____

Date: _____

Scripture Text:——————— Lesson Topic: _____

_____
_____
_____

Key Theme/Key Verse: _____

_____
_____
_____
_____

Thoughts from the Text: _____

_____
_____
_____
_____

How did this lesson impact my life? _____

_____
_____
_____
_____
_____

2ND QUARTER

Date: _____

Scripture Text:——————— Lesson Topic: _____

_____

_____

_____

Key Theme/Key Verse: _____

_____

_____

_____

_____

_____

Thoughts from the Text: _____

_____

_____

_____

_____

_____

How did this lesson impact my life?_____

_____

_____

_____

_____

_____

_____

Date: _____

Scripture Text:——————— Lesson Topic: _____

_____

_____

_____

Key Theme/Key Verse:_____

_____

_____

_____

_____

_____

Thoughts from the Text: _____

_____

_____

_____

_____

_____

How did this lesson impact my life?_____

_____

_____

_____

_____

_____

_____

2ND QUARTER

Date: _____

Scripture Text: —————— Lesson Topic: _____

_____

_____

_____

Key Theme/Key Verse: _____

_____

_____

_____

_____

_____

Thoughts from the Text: _____

_____

_____

_____

_____

_____

How did this lesson impact my life? _____

_____

_____

_____

_____

_____

Date: _____

Scripture Text:————————— Lesson Topic: _____

_____

_____

_____

Key Theme/Key Verse:_____

_____

_____

_____

_____

_____

Thoughts from the Text: _____

_____

_____

_____

_____

_____

How did this lesson impact my life?_____

_____

_____

_____

_____

_____

_____

2ND QUARTER

Date: _____

Scripture Text:——————— Lesson Topic: _____

_____

_____

_____

Key Theme/Key Verse: _____

_____

_____

_____

_____

_____

Thoughts from the Text: _____

_____

_____

_____

_____

_____

How did this lesson impact my life? _____

_____

_____

_____

_____

_____

Date: _____

Scripture Text: ————————— Lesson Topic: _____

_____

_____

_____

Key Theme/Key Verse: _____

_____

_____

_____

_____

_____

Thoughts from the Text: _____

_____

_____

_____

_____

_____

How did this lesson impact my life?_____

_____

_____

_____

_____

_____

_____

2ND QUARTER

Date: _____

Scripture Text:_____ Lesson Topic: _____

_____
_____
_____

Key Theme/Key Verse:_____

_____
_____
_____
_____
_____

Thoughts from the Text: _____

_____
_____
_____
_____
_____

How did this lesson impact my life?_____

_____
_____
_____
_____
_____
_____

NOTES

NOTES

Date: _____

Scripture Text: ———————— Lesson Topic: _____

_____

_____

_____

Key Theme/Key Verse: _____

_____

_____

_____

_____

Thoughts from the Text: _____

_____

_____

_____

_____

_____

How did this lesson impact my life? _____

_____

_____

_____

_____

_____

_____

3RD QUARTER

Date: _____

Scripture Text:_____ Lesson Topic: _____

_____

_____

_____

Key Theme/Key Verse:_____

_____

_____

_____

_____

Thoughts from the Text: _____

_____

_____

_____

_____

_____

How did this lesson impact my life?_____

_____

_____

_____

_____

_____

Date: _____

Scripture Text: —————— Lesson Topic: _____

_____
_____
_____

Key Theme/Key Verse: _____

_____
_____
_____
_____
_____

Thoughts from the Text: _____

_____
_____
_____
_____
_____

How did this lesson impact my life? _____

_____
_____
_____
_____
_____
_____

3RD QUARTER

Date: _____

Scripture Text:——————— Lesson Topic: _____

_____
_____
_____

Key Theme/Key Verse: _____

_____
_____
_____
_____
_____

Thoughts from the Text: _____

_____
_____
_____
_____
_____

How did this lesson impact my life? _____

_____
_____
_____
_____
_____
_____

Date: _____

Scripture Text:——————— Lesson Topic: _____

_____

_____

_____

Key Theme/Key Verse:_____

_____

_____

_____

_____

_____

Thoughts from the Text: _____

_____

_____

_____

_____

_____

How did this lesson impact my life?_____

_____

_____

_____

_____

_____

_____

Date: _____

Scripture Text:—————— Lesson Topic: _____

_____
_____
_____

Key Theme/Key Verse: _____

_____
_____
_____
_____
_____

Thoughts from the Text: _____

_____
_____
_____
_____
_____

How did this lesson impact my life? _____

_____
_____
_____
_____
_____
_____

Date: _____

Scripture Text:——————— Lesson Topic: _____

_____

_____

_____

Key Theme/Key Verse:_____

_____

_____

_____

_____

_____

Thoughts from the Text: _____

_____

_____

_____

_____

_____

How did this lesson impact my life?_____

_____

_____

_____

_____

_____

_____

3RD QUARTER

Date: _____

Scripture Text:—————— Lesson Topic: _____

_____

_____

_____

Key Theme/Key Verse:_____

_____

_____

_____

_____

_____

Thoughts from the Text: _____

_____

_____

_____

_____

_____

How did this lesson impact my life?_____

_____

_____

_____

_____

_____

Date: _____

Scripture Text: ——————— Lesson Topic: _____

_____

_____

_____

Key Theme/Key Verse: _____

_____

_____

_____

_____

_____

Thoughts from the Text: _____

_____

_____

_____

_____

_____

How did this lesson impact my life? _____

_____

_____

_____

_____

_____

_____

Date: _____

Scripture Text:————————— Lesson Topic: _____

_____
_____
_____

Key Theme/Key Verse:_____

_____
_____
_____
_____
_____

Thoughts from the Text: _____

_____
_____
_____
_____
_____

How did this lesson impact my life?_____

_____
_____
_____
_____
_____
_____

Date: _____

Scripture Text:——————— Lesson Topic: _____

_____

_____

_____

Key Theme/Key Verse:_____

_____

_____

_____

_____

_____

Thoughts from the Text: _____

_____

_____

_____

_____

_____

How did this lesson impact my life?_____

_____

_____

_____

_____

_____

_____

3RD QUARTER

Date: _____

Scripture Text:——————— Lesson Topic: _____

_____

_____

_____

Key Theme/Key Verse: _____

_____

_____

_____

_____

_____

Thoughts from the Text: _____

_____

_____

_____

_____

_____

How did this lesson impact my life?_____

_____

_____

_____

_____

_____

Date: _____

Scripture Text: —————— Lesson Topic: _____

_____

_____

_____

Key Theme/Key Verse: _____

_____

_____

_____

_____

_____

Thoughts from the Text: _____

_____

_____

_____

_____

_____

How did this lesson impact my life?_____

_____

_____

_____

_____

_____

_____

NOTES

NOTES

4TH QUARTER

Date: _____

Scripture Text:——————— Lesson Topic: _____

_____
_____
_____

Key Theme/Key Verse: _____

_____
_____
_____
_____
_____

Thoughts from the Text: _____

_____
_____
_____
_____
_____

How did this lesson impact my life? _____

_____
_____
_____
_____
_____
_____

Date: _____

Scripture Text:—————— Lesson Topic: _____

_____
_____
_____

Key Theme/Key Verse:_____

_____
_____
_____
_____
_____

Thoughts from the Text: _____

_____
_____
_____
_____
_____

How did this lesson impact my life?_____

_____
_____
_____
_____
_____
_____
_____

4TH QUARTER

Date: _____

Scripture Text: ——————— Lesson Topic: _____

_____

_____

_____

Key Theme/Key Verse: _____

_____

_____

_____

_____

_____

Thoughts from the Text: _____

_____

_____

_____

_____

_____

How did this lesson impact my life? _____

_____

_____

_____

_____

_____

_____

Date: _____

Scripture Text: ———————— Lesson Topic: _____

_____
_____
_____

Key Theme/Key Verse: _____

_____
_____
_____
_____
_____

Thoughts from the Text: _____

_____
_____
_____
_____
_____

How did this lesson impact my life? _____

_____
_____
_____
_____
_____
_____

4TH QUARTER

Date: _____

Scripture Text:————— Lesson Topic: _____

_____

_____

_____

Key Theme/Key Verse: _____

_____

_____

_____

_____

_____

Thoughts from the Text: _____

_____

_____

_____

_____

_____

How did this lesson impact my life? _____

_____

_____

_____

_____

_____

_____

Date: _____

Scripture Text:————————— Lesson Topic: _____

_____

_____

_____

Key Theme/Key Verse: _____

_____

_____

_____

_____

_____

Thoughts from the Text: _____

_____

_____

_____

_____

_____

How did this lesson impact my life? _____

_____

_____

_____

_____

_____

_____

Date: _____

Scripture Text:——————— Lesson Topic: _____

_____

_____

_____

Key Theme/Key Verse:_____

_____

_____

_____

_____

_____

Thoughts from the Text: _____

_____

_____

_____

_____

_____

How did this lesson impact my life?_____

_____

_____

_____

_____

_____

_____

Date: _____

Scripture Text:——————— Lesson Topic: _____

_____
_____
_____

Key Theme/Key Verse:_____

_____
_____
_____
_____
_____

Thoughts from the Text: _____

_____
_____
_____
_____
_____

How did this lesson impact my life?_____

_____
_____
_____
_____
_____
_____

4TH QUARTER

Date: _____

Scripture Text:——————— Lesson Topic: _____

_____

_____

_____

Key Theme/Key Verse:_____

_____

_____

_____

_____

_____

Thoughts from the Text: _____

_____

_____

_____

_____

_____

How did this lesson impact my life?_____

_____

_____

_____

_____

_____

_____

Date: _____

Scripture Text: _____ Lesson Topic: _____

_____

_____

_____

Key Theme/Key Verse: _____

_____

_____

_____

_____

_____

Thoughts from the Text: _____

_____

_____

_____

_____

_____

How did this lesson impact my life? _____

_____

_____

_____

_____

_____

_____

4TH QUARTER

Date: _____

Scripture Text: —————— Lesson Topic: _____

_____

_____

_____

Key Theme/Key Verse: _____

_____

_____

_____

_____

_____

Thoughts from the Text: _____

_____

_____

_____

_____

_____

How did this lesson impact my life? _____

_____

_____

_____

_____

_____

Date: _____

Scripture Text: —————— Lesson Topic: _____

_____

_____

_____

Key Theme/Key Verse: _____

_____

_____

_____

_____

_____

Thoughts from the Text: _____

_____

_____

_____

_____

_____

How did this lesson impact my life?_____

_____

_____

_____

_____

_____

_____

Date: _____

Scripture Text:———————— Lesson Topic: _____

_____

_____

_____

Key Theme/Key Verse: _____

_____

_____

_____

_____

_____

Thoughts from the Text: _____

_____

_____

_____

_____

_____

How did this lesson impact my life?_____

_____

_____

_____

_____

_____

_____

Date: _____

Scripture Text: ———————— Lesson Topic: _____

_____

_____

_____

Key Theme/Key Verse: _____

_____

_____

_____

_____

_____

Thoughts from the Text: _____

_____

_____

_____

_____

_____

How did this lesson impact my life? _____

_____

_____

_____

_____

_____

_____

Date: _____

Scripture Text:_____ Lesson Topic: _____

_____

_____

_____

Key Theme/Key Verse:_____

_____

_____

_____

_____

_____

Thoughts from the Text: _____

_____

_____

_____

_____

_____

How did this lesson impact my life?_____

_____

_____

_____

_____

_____

_____

NOTES